This
Sleepy Little Yoga book
belongs to

. . . .

To Liberty Rose with love – R. W.

For my grandson Jacob John – M. S.

SLEEPY LITTLE YOGA

A HUTCHINSON BOOK 978 0 091 89350 7 (from January 2007)

0 091 89350 X

Published in Great Britain by Hutchinson,
an imprint of Random House Children's Books.

This edition published 2007

1 3 5 7 9 10 8 6 4 2

Text copyright © Rebecca Whitford, 2007
Illustrations copyright © Martina Selway, 2007
Photographs © Hutchinson Children's Books, 2007
Photographs by Micaela Cianci

The right of Rebecca Whitford and Martina Selway to be identified as the author and illustrator
of this work has been asserted in accordance with the Copyright, Designs and Patents Act 1988.

RANDOM HOUSE CHILDREN'S BOOKS
A division of the Random House Group Ltd,
London, Sydney, Auckland, Johannesburg and agencies throughout the world

THE RANDOM HOUSE GROUP Limited Reg. No. 954009

www.kidsatrandomhouse.co.uk

A CIP catalogue record for this book is available from the British Library

Printed in Singapore

Sleepy Little Yoga

Rebecca Whitford & Martina Selway

HUTCHINSON

LONDON SYDNEY AUCKLAND JOHANNESBURG

Yoga Baby...

hangs upside down like a

eee-eeek

bat

Yoga Baby . . .

blinks her eyes like an

to-wit to-woo

owl

Yoga Baby . . .

sniffs the night air like a

sniff sniff

little fox

Yoga Baby...

flops down like a

aaaah

tired bunny

Yoga Baby...

pushes his feet to the stars like a

ooooooooh-ah

bear cub

Yoga Baby . . .

curls up like a

snuffle

little hedgehog

Yoga Baby...

hums like a

mmmmm

sleepy bee

Yoga Baby...

floats down like a

flitter flutter

dreamy moth

Yoga Baby
drifts away

Z Z Z Z

on a cloud
through the night

★ Sleepy Little Yoga ★

A Note to Parents and Carers

Sleepy Little Yoga is a gentle and relaxing yoga sequence to help toddlers wind down before bed time or nap time — either by copying Yoga Baby and the night-time animals, by practising with a grown-up, or by simply reading and sharing. The poses include calming Forward Bends that 'quieten the energies' and are often practised towards the end of the day; Palming the Eyes, which is very restful; and Bee Breath, which is a soothing breathing technique often used to combat insomnia. With practice, yoga can help to calm and relax toddlers by encouraging moments of quiet and stillness.

Sleepy Little Yoga is designed to be fun and relaxing, not as a manual, so allow it to take its own form and give your child lots of encouragement.

Practice tips:

• Practise with bare feet on a non-slip surface; use a clear space in a warm room and both you and your child should wear loose, comfortable clothes — pyjamas are perfect for this.

• Like any form of exercise it is best not to practise this sequence immediately after eating.

• Practise with your child so that he or she can copy you.

• Use your own judgement with your child's ability and let your child move at his or her own pace, giving support where necessary.

• Encourage your child into poses but do not look for or expect perfection. Most of all **Sleepy Little Yoga** is meant to be a fun, positive experience.

• Don't force your toddler into a pose or let him or her hold any pose for too long.

• Allow your child to play around with a pose before moving on to the next one.

• Simple stories can help your Yoga Baby relax when in the resting pose.

• The photos overleaf are not precise because they are a real reflection of how our toddlers have interpreted the poses!

Most importantly, keep your **Sleepy Little Yoga** practice **laid-back** and **gentle!**

Explanation of Poses

Bat (Wide Forward Bend) — from a wide-legged standing position raise arms up, then bend at the hips, letting arms, hands and the upper body relax down to the floor. Keep knees bent if more comfortable. Uncurl slowly back to a standing position.

Owl (Palming the Eyes) — sit back on heels with a straight spine and eyes wide open. Open and close the eyes two or three times. Rub palms together in front of the chest to create warmth, then lower the head and place the palms over the eyes. Stay until the warmth fades, then repeat.

Fox (Kneeling Forward Bend) — from sitting on heels, move up onto knees while sweeping arms up above the head. Then stretch up with palms facing each other. Lift the chin and look up.

Bunny (Swan) — from fox pose, sinking hips/bottom onto heels, bend forward and lower chest to thighs and forehead to the floor with arms outstretched. Hold and relax.

Bear cub (Upward Raised Legs) — from a lying position, draw knees in over the chest, place arms alongside the body with the palms down. Raise heels up towards the ceiling and try to keep chin tucked in. Bend the knees in and repeat.

Hedgehog (Knees to chest) — from bear cub pose, hug knees to chest then move the head and upper body towards the knees, try to keep chin tucked in, then relax down to the floor.

Bee (Bee Breath) — from a sitting position bend the knees, bring the soles of the feet together and sit with a straight spine. Rest the back of the hands on the knees, close the eyes and breathe in through the nose. Keeping the lips gently closed, breathe out with a slow, steady hum — 'mmmm'. Breathe in again and repeat several times.

Moth (Cobbler) — from a sitting position with bent knees and the soles of the feet together, hold the toes, sit up with a straight spine, bend the elbows and fold forwards, relaxing the head towards the feet. Relax knees out to the side. Gently move knees back together and sit up.

Rest (Savasana) — lie down on back, keeping body in a straight line. Have legs hip-width apart and let feet relax out to the sides. Keep arms away from the body, and the palms turned up. Try to keep head in line with the spine. Close the eyes and imagine drifting on a cloud through the night, past the moon and the stars . . .

Bat (Wide Forward Bend)

Owl (Palming the Eyes)

Bunny (Swan)

Fox (Kneeling Forward Bend)

Bear cub (Upward Raised Legs)

Hedgehog (Knees to chest)

Bee (Bee Breath)

Moth (Cobbler)

Rest (Savasana)